WATER AND SKY

For Kate

WATER AND SKY

VOICES FROM THE RIVERSIDE

NEIL SENTANCE

Caught by the River

LITTLE TOLLER

Foreword

Neil Sentance writes about his native Lincolnshire riverlands with the blend of toughness and tenderness that readers who know England's working country people will recognise as a defining characteristic. The combination is found in his worldview, in his lyric descriptions of landscape, and in the characters that he brings out from the backstage of history to address us from the River Witham's banks. It is there, for example, in the martins 'skimming over the water' with 'curvilinear wings the colour of sump oil', and in his tale of the paranoid grandfather who thinks he is being robbed when he is struck on the head by a can of beans. It is also there, heartbreakingly so, in the decision of his other grandfather to sell his farm when he realises that 'the old country attributes of hard work and patience were no longer enough in an era of paper mountains, aggressive marketing and diminishing returns'. Such cruel – and comic, and edifying – effects of passing time are everywhere in *Water and Sky*, and using his different keys Sentance employs them to communicate far more than conventional rural nostalgia.

In *Water and Sky* Sentance revisits the walks of his childhood, and tells a story of the land around the River Witham through memoir, biography, 'family lore' and what could be called psychogeographic drift. He evokes a sense of transition from a rural culture based on meaningful work to one of leisure and commodification, but rather than lament a lost Golden Age, he celebrates the countryside's muddy reclamations of modernity. Anyone who grew up in or near a British market town, as I did, will recognise places like Swallow's Mill, the water mill that 'by the seventies had been converted into a nightclub, entered by the gates just past the tractor company' and whose revellers 'would row in small boats down from the Saltersford Bridge on Somerby Hill and row back again, sculling upstream, after a night of partying in their polyester finery'. On the dry, chalk Wolds it was tractors not boats, but it comes to the same thing; as with the children's play on the river, or the farmers using leisure trips to Holland to inspect their rivals' husbandry, this is the anti-chocolate box countryside, but distinct and even idyllic nonetheless.

Sentance's democracy and realism are of course – as he says of one of his stories – in the Thomas Hardy tradition of English writing about the countryside. However, when I first read his writing on the Caught by the River website, that 1970s nightclub brought to mind another reference, in Psalm 137, the main source of the Rivers of Babylon lyric: by the river where we sat down and wept when we remembered. The link might seem grandiose or superficial depending on whether you have the Bible, The Melodians or Boney M in mind, but to me those words seem relevant to the writing in the second half of this book, in which Neil recalls childhood summers on his grandfather's farm and then his final tour on the eve of the sale.

I have a particular interest in this because, as I wrote in *The Farm*, in my early 30s I had to help my father, brother and mother lay out and sell our family's farm when agricultural economics did for them, too. I had grown up on the slightly ramshackle, nineteenth-century farmstead that in some ways resembles Sentance's grandfather's, and many of the beautifully evoked details – the barns like ships 'anchored over swells of wheat and barley', the 'fantastical cobwebs looped in high corners', and the 'ancient bulb hanging from a thin braided cord, rimed in straw dust and casting a buttery half-light' – feel entirely familiar to me. Also familiar are his grandfather's feelings of confused resignation and self-blame. Farmers like this have been encouraged to subject their personal, tender feelings to the tough realities of life and markets, which is one reason why the loss of more than 300,000 of these farms since 1939 has not been more acknowledged or mourned. Sentance's writing is never explicitly political, but in his personal meditation and his depiction of the culture of which these businesses are part, he makes a strong case for their better treatment by people who make the laws that govern our so-called free markets.

In recent years an increasing number of people have begun to wonder if we might do something better with the countryside than turn it into a series of giant suburban leisure parks set among anonymous large-scale farms. Writing like this, as well as being compelling in its own right, should be part of that wondering. Tender and tough, ideal and real, past and present, do not have to be polarised; we are beginning to find that in some cases, blending them will work too. These voices from the riverside remind us of why it is worth trying. How shall we sing the Lord's song in a Strange Land? Like this, perhaps, among martins the colour of sump oil and men rowing boats to night clubs in water mills; like this, somewhere between the poetry and the prose, the water and the sky, the tender and tough.

Richard Benson
London, 2013

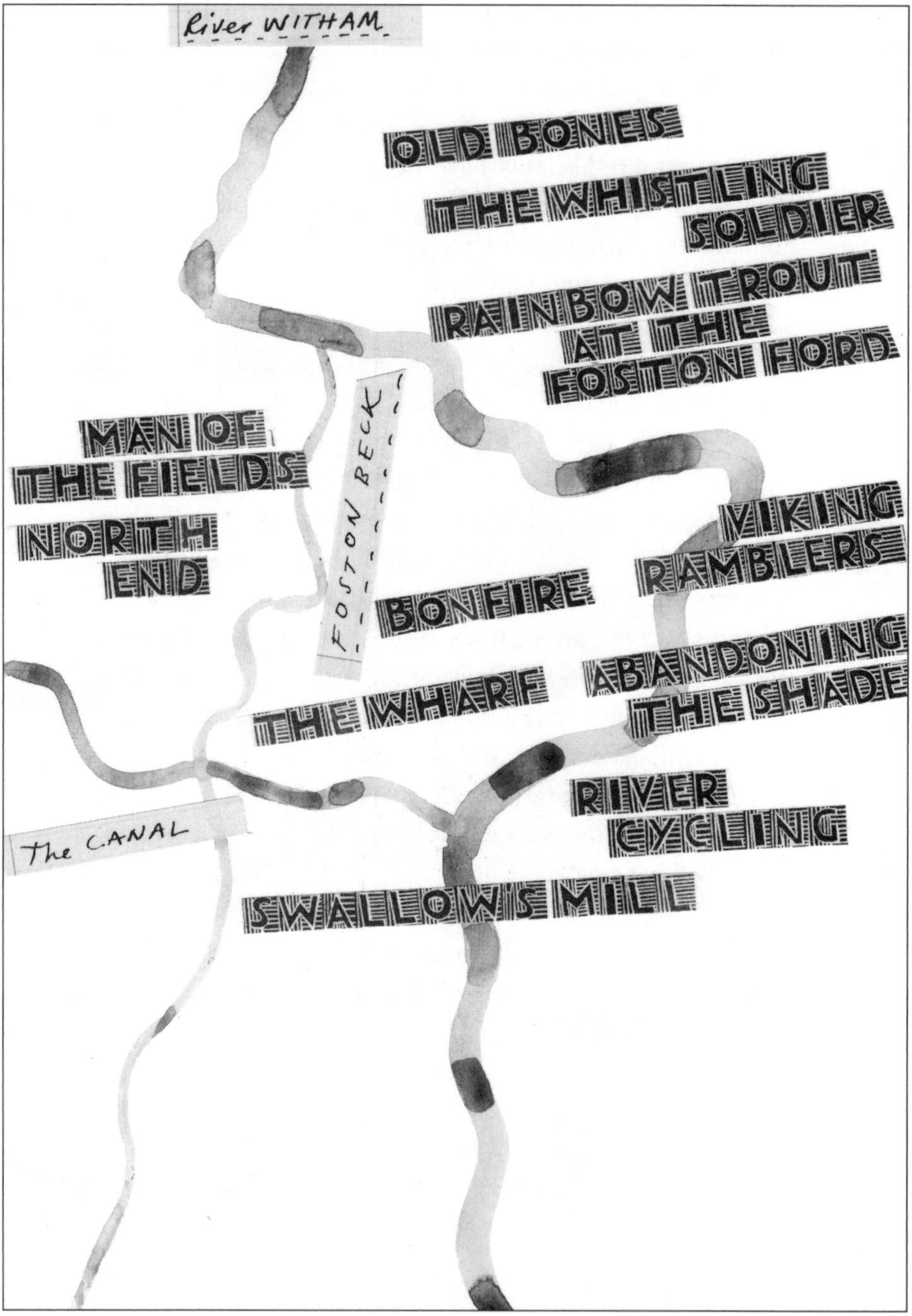

River WITHAM

OLD BONES

THE WHISTLING
SOLDIER

RAINBOW TROUT
AT THE
FOSTON FORD

MAN OF
THE FIELDS

NORTH
END

FOSTON BECK

VIKING
RAMBLERS

BONFIRE

ABANDONING
THE SHADE

THE WHARF

RIVER
CYCLING

The CANAL

SWALLOWS MILL

Contents

Town River

1980
Abandoning the Shade

I grew up a few streets away from the River Witham, and though I haven't lived there for many years, belonging has a steadfast grip. It was a place of mossy banks and murky water, where sunburnt summer kids played among the shoals and riffles, piratical with wooden swords, dangling from one bank to the other on tyre-and-rope swings – Dad even made me a buccaneer's dagger, a snickersnee, from our washing-line prop, much to my mother's annoyance. We'd go fishing in Wyndham Park, catching glimpses of the rare native white-clawed crayfish in the pools near the inflow of the culverted Mowbrook, and watching the swales of martins skimming over the water, their curvilinear wings the colour of sump oil. House sparrows teemed in the hawthorn, so common as to almost go unnoticed. Sometimes I'd take my 1960s copy of *The Observer's Book of Birds*, re-covered in brown paper and re-bound with electrical tape, but mostly I'd be deep into the day-long games of cricket in the bankside pastures, where the fielders bounded into the river like eager dogs and countless balls were lost in the reeds.

In winter, taking the riverside walk edged by wind-rattled trees, we would make our way past the telephone exchange to London Road football ground, now predictably the site of a supermarket. Then it was a three-sided near-derelict stadium built on the floodplain and open on the south side, where the cricket square was roped off. Every other weekend we would watch Town struggle in the mid-reaches of the Northern Premier or the Midland Leagues. We'd skitter over the dilapidated wooden stands in the glare of the looming new floodlights, until the old men who'd been sitting in the decaying seats every Saturday since before the war would bellow at us to pack it in. Adding our small straining voices to the roars of the crowd, a few hundred die-hards too stubborn or hard up to go to Forest or County, we'd shout for an hour and a half, till our throats were raw and rasping behind tight-wound scarves. The river received its share of footballs booted out of the ground by a lumbering centre-half – sometimes you'd see them there bobbing like buoys in the dusklight on the walk home.

Now and then we would cross town to the Canal, sleeving its way to Nottingham, where Alan Sillitoe writes of undefeated Arthur Seaton fishing from the towpath at the end of *Saturday Night and Sunday Morning*: 'whenever you caught a fish, the fish caught you'. More often as not, we'd cross over the Bridge End Road, past the river mill, and into Dysart Park, and take a dip in the lido, where several generations of the family had learnt to swim. The water was as cold as a mountain rill. Dead flies or exhausted beetles floated on the wavering surface – we would mount rescue missions, mostly in an effort to stave off the chill. From there we would take the primrose path up Cold Harbour Lane to the Hills and Hollows, along stony tracks and through kissing gates, up to where hawks soared and newly-colonising collared doves called day-long in the spinneys. From the high terrace paths we could see over to Beacon Hill, which had carried firelight messages in the pre-modern age, and Belton House, serene in its parkland, and through the Witham gap to the white cooling towers on the Trent. Up here, among the redbrick ruins of Walters's farm, we once found a bird's nest inside a rusted tangle of farm machinery. Old shepherd huts were left stranded under hedgerows, wormy sides collapsed in on themselves, corroded iron wheels now sank into the soil. Pungent tiers of wild garlic clouded the banks of thigh-high stinging nettles. We were the warriors of the hill, fearless wayfarers, but we soon got to know where dock leaves were to be found.

Reaching back to childhood now, I look through a dust-covered window. As Laurie Lee says in 'The Abandoned Shade', his poem of childhood memory: 'the voice of the boy, the boy I seek, within my mouth is dumb'. But the writer Bruce Chatwin often recounted Proust's notion that the walks of our childhood provide 'the substance of our "mental soil" – to which for ever after we are bound'. For me, it's a soil warmed by a quiet sun and cut through by the shining river.

1975
Swallow's Mill

The river ran into Swallow's Mill, just over the road from Dad's old house. In the fifties, there were lock gates here controlling the flow of water. It was the job of the lock-keeper to maintain an even flow and not let the river flood the bankside houses, as had happened years before. With fine nominative determinism the lock-keeper was a Mr Brooks, 'Brookie' to the kids of the river, whom he'd help fish for tiddlers under the bridge, putting them in jam jars and then back in the water at the day's end. But by the seventies the mill had been converted into a nightclub, entered by the gates just past the tractor company. The mill wheel had been made into a feature, visible behind a glass front from the dance floor, and still turning at something less than vinyl speed. I remember sitting at the top of the stairs at home on a Saturday night as Dad, impish in his wide-lapelled brown leather jacket, got ready to take Mum there, she beautiful in home-tailored costumes made from Saturday market material. Other revellers would row in small boats down from the Saltersford Bridge on Somerby Hill and row back again, sculling upstream, after a night of partying in their polyester finery. Sometimes there would be a turn from a long-faded star, Trini Lopez once, Dad said, backed by the clinking cadences of the river below. Or maybe strutting local lads like Vince Eager, from the Larry

Parnes stable of early British rockers, still dreaming of the 2I's Coffee Bar, and Brian 'Licorice' Locking, onetime bassist with The Shadows, back in town now the summer holiday of the sixties had ended.

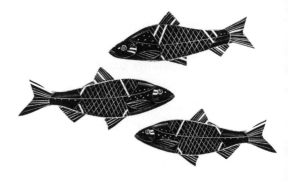

1955
River Cycling and other 'Stunts'

After the war all the riverside houses had long gardens and people tended vegetable plots that reached to the banks. When they needed water they would use a stirrup pump with a long hosepipe and draw from the river into the gardens. No doubt this contributed to the low midsummer water levels, down to 12 inches or less. Willows drooped low over the surface like shawled old ladies, their slender tendrils hiding warring coots, and breaking the waterline and generating micro-eddies. For the local kids this was their playground and they would do all sorts of 'stunts'. Stan Hood, one of the older lads, was the leader, running wild as his dad worked away as a cooper in the breweries of Burton-on-Trent. Carrying the younger ones across the river on big stepping stones lumped from the quarry up the road, he sometimes jumped in, drenching them both. He was like the mythical scorpion that stings the frog carrying it across the stream – it was just in his nature. He'd throw magnesium flares at the other kids' feet, just to upskittle them. In the disused lemonade factory at the end of the terrace, he instituted a pinching candle rite for membership of his mob. In the winters, his gang roller-skated in the snow, up the wide paths of Somerby Hill, ringing doorbells and hightailing away. Householders were ready for it – to escape the kids had to climb the five-bar gates of Swallow's

Mill, still on skates. Stan always wore a faded pin-stripe suit, but his teenage disciples would never say in earshot that he'd had to stay up all night to paint on the lines. 'Soft as grease', Dad said, but he enjoyed being one of this motley crowd, the borough rough element.

Dad was always happy whittling a shard of wood. He once spent weeks making a toy yacht, honed on a spoke-shave, then launched with fanfare from an embayed island in the stream. But the string broke on the maiden voyage and it drifted downstream and rapidly out of reach. Another time he rigged ex-ministry telephones from one side of the river to the other, ringing Fabian of the Yard, Whitehall 1212. Maybe that was the same day that Alan Briggs's sister put her head through the iron railings of the bridge and got it stuck. Her dad had to come and get her out with a crowbar – the railings remained there, deformed, for years until eventually a lorry lost control coming down the hill, hit the bridge and sent the whole lot plummeting into the river.

In the winter Dad and his best friend Ian would skate along the river and then up Spittlegate Hill, following the snow plough to Harrowby Hall. In the summer though they spent their days on bikes, riding through the low turbid river water and under the bridge towards the mill, deaf to the angry shouts of older lads fishing with split-cane rods for trout. And then up the bank and off into the country, back to the river's younger self, to the dens of Robbers Rocks and past the vast cetacean jawbone placed on the roadside that gave its name to Whalebone Lane, and beyond, along the High Dyke to Woodnook valley, freedom transmitted with every derailleur gearshift.

Other times they would follow the spring line up Halls Hill, windy heights above the town where Dad as a young lad had put stones in his pockets, thinking he'd be blown into Leicestershire. Or a detour to Monkey Millard's Lane

– old Millard had once brought some monkeys back from a trip abroad and kept them in heated outbuildings on the farm until in a power cut one cold winter night they all froze to death. One summer Dad found an old motorbike in Millard's field and managed to get it going, larruped in engine oil, he said. The old man took off the front wheel in an attempt to forestall these high-jinks but Dad replaced it with a wheelbarrow wheel and raced over the rutted tracks and through swards of rough meadow grass and cornflowers, round the stands of pollarded oaks, until the petrol ran out or the dusk descended with the swifts screaming over the barn roofs.

1949
Bonfire

For my father, the best night of the year was 5th November, Bonfire Night. He would build up the bonfire for weeks before on the river bank, piling up kindling and windfall branches from the park, adding cast-off Victorian washstands stripped of their marble tops and huge rosewood chests of drawers left unsold at the market, alongside any flammable detritus from the still weed-strewn bombsites off Bridge End Road. Then came the big event – Dad's sister made the Guy, stuffed with the *News of the World*, and people from all around would turn out. Grandad, who had been the local ARP warden and fireman during the war, was in charge of lighting and controlling the fire – nothing happened till he came home from working on the Lipton's van mobile shop. Brown-suited, always well-shod in patent leather shoes with spats, his black lacquered hair waved back from his high brow, he would go about the lighting without fuss, pencil stub behind his ear, woodbine in top pocket, or vice versa, never sure which would find his mouth first. Then he'd strike the match, the first flames crackling at the tinder line, and the fire grew, a heat-haze penumbra flickering up the side of the vaulted kilns of the maltings on the opposite bank.

Grandad would then let the fireworks off, not so many, just enough to rip the sky with a booming blast of coppery sparks. Afterwards, everyone would pick out their roast potatoes from the belly of the fire, and natter with mouths full. Dad would watch the line-graven faces of the grown-ups shining in the ember light. Nearing midnight, folks would start to clear up, and then walk off home happy, a few hours sleep ahead before the factory hooter next morning.

Dad would look on, hands deep in his pockets as the cold bit, as Grandad went methodically about the closing rites. Pushing the dwindled fire into the Witham with the tip of his holiday shoes, the smouldering remains would die with a brief hiss. The seams of ash and lumps of clinkered wood sank beneath the waterline and washed under the arch of the bridge, away downriver and into the soot-black night. Grandad would take Dad's hand and without a word walk back through the gate of the river house.

1985
Viking Ramblers

I found a bleached colour photograph of Bob and Joe in an old glue-stuck album. It's from the early 1970s. They have cigarettes on the go, Players Navy Cut most likely, and are standing by a blue Ford in fading sunlight. As they blink into the camera, they don't look much like brothers. Bob is dark, angular and lean, brilliantined hair swept back from a high forehead. Joe is stocky and fair-skinned, hair white-grey and cut short, military fashion. They look nonchalant, ageing men nearing retirement, loafing in worsted Sunday suits. They seem at ease with each other and the sumpy and vulcanised reek of the old cars they drive and tend at the weekends. They've never had much money but never known much want either. They smoke their fags, have outings on the weekend, see the grandkids, go to the agricultural show. Sunday dinner out is with the missus, occasionally tea at the new British Home Stores café in Nottingham. In summer there are social trips to Skegness – the bus stops en route at the Three Kings, the medieval pub at Threekingham (where three Danish sovereigns were slain in 869). Numbers are chalked on the bus wheels and whoever pulls the number out of a hat that accords with the pub stop, wins the kitty. Otherwise they rarely stray far from home, that last generation of stayers. But they've seen plenty of life through staying put.

They were born on the moor, in the first village (once a Viking hill colony) on the Great North Road a mile out of town, within a year or two of each other during the First World War. There were abundant other brothers and sisters too, living cheek by jowl in a small ironstone cottage in Pond Street, not far from the site of a Civil War battlefield – the legend was that Cromwell had lodged next door. Their old man had once been a professional soldier, and took the King's shilling as far as South Africa, but came home after the Great War and settled to working the land, as so many before him. As kids Bob and Joe often cycled down the lane to the Witham, now forming a skittish serpentine curve through the parklands on the northern edge of town. Here they had some hard-won seclusion, away from the cramped concessions of home. They played at the Hollow Ponds, natural spring-fed tarns bordered by tall thickets of reeds, a good hiding place. They tinkered with their bikes, propped up against ancient alders, deer-gnarled and rugged trees out of place in a park of exotic plantations of horse chestnut and lime. Fishing the ponds a little, when the estate men weren't around, they mostly just talked and smoked by the paths, lives absorbed in football and engine oil.

As they grew up, they might have gone home via one of the three inns on the High Street, limestone-built alehouses all known locally as the 'top, middle and bottom' and never by their real names, but there was scant money for ale. Then along Green Street to the meadows known as the Wong, where livestock were once gathered prior to the journey to market, and home to Pond Street via a footpath by the Hemplands village green, or by way of Spring End where upwellings fed the pond at the junction with the High Street. Years later, it was here that Joe, escaping the police, drove his motorbike into the water, jumping off at the last moment, rodeo fashion. He had used an old Oxo cube label in the road tax disc holder (at that time they looked very similar to the real thing), but a copper had clocked him and chased him down Whipperstall Hill and Beggars Lane. Joe would have loved the chase. Reaching the pond, he submerged the Norton so it was out of sight and sauntered off home. Next day he retrieved the bike and dried the engine parts in his mother's oven range overnight. This was their patch. Every nook of the landscape was a token of their story.

By this time, Bob was apprenticed at Parkers the Bakers, delivering loaves on his three-speed bike. A member of one of the cycling clubs so widespread then, on sunny weekends off he'd keep the bike on the road, doing the 120-mile round trip to the east coast for a swift hour of bracing sea air. Once he cycled many miles to see a race; feeling tired on arrival he fell asleep and missed the whole spectacle. Married at twenty-two, he became the mobile shop driver for Liptons the grocers. He settled down and moved into town, a damp end terrace house on Bridge End Road by the Witham, where his son, my father, was born on a wartime January Saturday.

The line of the upper Witham snakes along the borderlands with Nottinghamshire before breaking out at the limestone escarpment at the Lincoln Gap, then forms the arc of an unlucky inverted horseshoe that hangs on the hook of the county town at Brayford Pool. In our town, twenty miles upriver, it may have been a navigational aid for German planes. Bombs dropped all over town, the Luftwaffe aiming for the Hornsby tank armaments plant or RAF Bomber Command's No 5 Group at St Vincent's House just up the hill (where later the famous Dambuster raids were devised) or the East Coast railway line. The long rows of drab Victorian terraces smearing out from the slums of Witham Place towards the cemetery under Halls Hill endured many raids. A backyard Anderson shelter a few streets away suffered a direct hit. Clumps of rosebay willow herb, the fireweed, thrived in the bombed out gaps among smashed brick walls and splintered timber, and blood-red wall valerian grew out of twisted iron bedroom fireplaces left stranded and exposed mid-air. Bob's house survived, only losing the odd windowpane and roof slate, the river waters always close at hand for dowsing incendiaries. Bob often later said the river had saved the family several times over. The Witham was his talisman, at the time he needed one most.

Deemed unfit for active service, after work Bob drove a lend-lease American ambulance. Then there were nights on ARP warden duty. On his Monday afternoon off, he'd drive an undertaker's hearse. The levels of exhaustion are hard now to comprehend. His main hobby, shared with Joe, was tinkering with old cars. He'd acquired a run-down 1929 Triumph, but after Coventry was destroyed by bombing in November 1940, spare car parts were hard to come by. But Joe was some kind of improvisational genius and fixed it up, and they laid up the wheel-less car on bricks in the allotment next to the Witham, waiting for the better times. Joe moonlighted from his factory job as a cinema projector at the Empire Theatre, when it was still gas-lit and unelectrified. The projector had a petrol-driven generator. Joe, of course, siphoned off the petrol for his motorbike and the generator would run out of fuel during a film, stopping it mid-reel, catcalls ringing out in the dark. But his carefree life changed when on his bike he was hit by a drunk-driver. After months in hospital, he emerged a wreck of a man, forever after with a nervous shake. I remember him now, bent uneasily over a motor part, his hand trembling over the head of a screw. It was painful to watch. He'd get there in the end – 'never is a long day', he'd say – and there would be a heavy moment of stillness as the screwdriver at last engaged with the cross-head. Air seemed to rush back into our lungs.

In the polar winter of 1947 Bob delivered groceries to the far-flung Withamside villages that were otherwise cut-off. Snow drifted up to the top of telegraph poles in an arctic spell lasting, he remembered, eight weeks and three days. The flatlands beyond the Witham source at Blue Point were also counterpaned in snow. But the Fenlanders struggled to feed families and farm stock. At Skillington, near where the river rises, buses and trucks stopped off the main road at the Blue Horse Inn and left engines running all night to stop the diesel solidifying in the fuel tanks. Bob drove into the village knowing he might not be able to get out. He remembered the eleventh-century church was white-towered, flat pale light refracting through the iced-over stained glass. After Bob dealt out the rations, his van was stuck in the snow and it took farm labourers working for hours in a whirling blizzard to dig it out again. Then he went on, in the waning daylight, to the village of South Witham where the river was held fast by ice. Here Bob tried to thaw out in the Angel Inn, fortified with tots of rum supplied by the blind landlord, before attempting the long trip back. The country folks remembered him ever after. Years later, and always worried about the van's cash takings, he developed a fear of being robbed. Coming back into town down Spittlegate Hill one day he felt the heavy thud of a blunt object hit him on the back of the head. He stopped and turned, ready to confront his assailant – a tin of baked beans rolled along the van floor having been dislodged from the shelf.

It is the winter of 1985. I wheel the bike out from the shed. It is a Viking Rambler, ten-speed gears, burnt-orange frame, racing handlebars. I strike out into the silent lanes in a land of heavy clay. Some fields are stippled with blackened stalks of burnt stubble; others are just long shallow declivities of rich soil, picked over by small flocks of sheltering lapwings. Wind-bent lone trees stand tall on the horizon. I head out down the school lane, into the low sun, past the council houses and the wellfield cricket pitch. The hedgerows are still deep at this time, in this part of the Midlands. I go past the footpath that cuts through the middle of cornfields to the gentrifying pub, until lately a sawdust-floored farmworkers' inn, now a chintzy eatery for the newly monied. I turn down the back lane and bike alongside the trickling West Glen River, a tributary of the greater fenland river, the Welland. Rabbit-cropped downlands are beyond the ditch. Sometimes I bike up a gravel track to The Lodge, a tumbledown Victorian cottage romantically sited on its own hill, or up to the pond, where my uncle fishes while smoking his liquorice-paper roll-ups. But today, I go past the small stone cottage with the pictures of John Wayne and Jimmy Stewart in the window, the home on the range, and keep going, feeling the wind at my back, and cycle faster past the peafields and droving tracks. I reach the Roman road, the High Dyke, and onwards under the London–Edinburgh railway line, and through to Woolsthorpe. I get to Skillington and cross the Cringle brook and then over the county border, seeing the yellow and black insignia of the Viking Way on a gatepost. This was a favourite Sunday drive when I was small. I think of the tender grandfather Bob and great-uncle Joe who took me on these trips, and later to the football and Trent Bridge Test matches, taught me snooker and billiards and kept me and my brothers supplied in sweets and dandelion-and-burdock. They had both died in the last few weeks. They left behind their stories of this place, their place in it. The breeze gets up and dust rises off the fields as I wheel the bike around and turn for home.

1957
The Wharf

The Witham is navigable only in its lower reaches,
from Brayford Pool at Lincoln to the Haven at
Boston, where it flows into the Wash. The Romans
used the river to transport goods in bulk and built the Foss
Dyke Navigation to link the Witham to the Trent. The upper
Witham, however, has never been an industrial conduit and
its banks are lined by woodlands, allotments, horse paddocks,
scrublands, old orchards and cattle pastures. But during the
first tumults of the Industrial Revolution the river's lack of
commercial utility led to the construction of the Canal, built
in the 1790s to carry coal from Nottingham to the new roaring
furnaces of our town. It remained operational until the 1920s.
Sections of the canal have been restored in recent decades by
dedicated volunteer groups and the inland water authorities.
On one stretch, at Woolsthorpe wharf, stands the former
boatman's pub, the Rutland Arms, aka the Dirty Duck. As a
teenager in the 1980s, with a bunch of schoolmates, I often
pitched a tent here by an old boat repair yard and the vestigial
ribs of an upturned icebreaker, and unsteadily learnt to drink
Batemans amber pale ale and shoot pool in a dim backroom.
Walking along the towpath in springtime we drifted through
clouds of wildflowers and thickets of long grasses, catching
burrs on our jeans. Once we saw a grass snake glide sinuously
from bank to bank. Whorls of pondweed and water plantain

greened the surface – on a twilight walk, I remember it dappled with velvet shadows, the air thrumming with overflying odonates, gauze-winged dragonflies and damselflies, and the buzzing chatter of my mates. Canoes and narrowboats swept along to the winding holes, broad pools constructed as turning circles for watercraft, steering clear of tangled sunken forests of reeds colonised by chubb. Anglers cast for the pike that lurked among the duckweed, 'killers from the egg: the malevolent aged grin. . .'

But a search today for the canal's urban starting point gives up only a relic, a fenced scrapyard long sited on the filled-in canal basin. The basin is marked on old OS maps, occupying the same place as the town's first railway station. In the early nineteenth century this would have been the hub of the borough's burgeoning industries, especially brewery maltings, but the canal trade gradually declined after the advent of the railways. Enterprising locals then hired out rowing boats at the wharf and the basin became a venue for community gatherings and jamborees. Even the Skegness lifeboat was unveiled here before the boat's fifty-mile onward journey overland to the coast. My grandmother remembered her father attaching ice blades to his hobnail boots and skating along the canal during the winter freezes before the First World War, thirty miles and more to the Trent at West Bridgford, 'under the magical presidency of Jack Frost' in Roger Deakin's memorable phrase. The winter was my great-grandfather's chance for a high day and holiday, for the thrill of zooming on the ice, stopping by at the Rutland Arms or the Peacock at Redmile or the Anchor at Plungar: come the spring, he'd be hitching up his pony and trap and touring the Fens for the potato crops that he'd sell on to army camps, prisons and the newfangled Smiths Crisps factory down in Cricklewood. But following the closure of the canal in 1929, the wharf's tall Italianate granaries were torn down and the basin plugged and covered over, and the site became one of lost industrial archaeology, another municipal ghost in a town of many.

Old Wharf Road, the route to the old basin, still runs under the railway arch, half-forgotten on the edge of the town centre. It's a dingy lane beside the main Nottingham road, all flat-faced industrial sheds and gimcrack builders' merchant compounds, achromatic except for the vivid yellow ragwort and dandelions extruding from cracked pavings, and graffiti tags daubed on corrugated garage doors. I worked in a hemp sack factory here during student holidays and remember bleak break-times, longed-for and fleeting, huddled under the archway. Just beyond here still stand the old auction rooms, ironstone-fronted, Midland redbrick-backed, modest single-storey warehouse survivors of the canal's golden age. In December 1956, my father, a few weeks shy of fifteen, started work here as a market porter and booking clerk. Forestalled in his ambition to become a motor mechanic by the fuel shortages triggered by the Suez crisis, he took this unpromising job as a means of escaping a return to school the following January. Soon, though, he grew to like the work, mingling with on-the-make antique dealers and scrap merchants, hayseed market gardeners and farmers.

Aside from farm valuations and sales, his employers held monthly furniture sales and the Saturday market. Dad would get to the Old Wharf Road saleyard early and use a large pair of wheels to move into place a vast cumbrous chiffonier cupboard. This was for the Nottingham cheesemonger, who'd sell ripe wedges of Stilton and Red Cheddar arrayed on its stained rosewood top. The rest of the morning Dad would book in items for the sales that began when his boss rang an old brass bell at midday – first, the pigs, ushered down Wide Westgate in a cascade of squeals. After that came the tool auction – sheds, homemade ironing boards, rusting garden implements, mowers and pre-war cars. Across the road, the potato sale started, great sacks of spuds heaped against a wall like rubble. Later were the house clearances, the best stuff cherry-picked for the grander monthly midweek sales, and thus often on Saturdays left only with the dregs, the 'rammel' in local parlance – broken cutlery, mouldy curtains, moth-eaten rugs, sagging old chairs and de-sprung sofas that would be bought, re-covered, repaired and resold at the next market. Also bicycles, of all types. A Mr Curtis of Billingborough would buy job lots and cart them back to his workshop, stacked precariously on the roof rack of his car. Ever trying to supplement his low wage, Dad would sometimes buy a bike too, bidding under the cipher name of 'Briggs of Bottesford', and recondition it at home for resale. Occasionally he'd buy a row of old bedroom washstands no longer needed with the rise of indoor plumbing and convert them into drawing tables: a schoolteacher he knew would pay four shillings for their marble tops for her pupils to make clay models on; the wooden legs and frames might then be chopped up for tinder sticks. Once he built a crude roulette wheel to sell, copied from the cowboy matinees he'd seen at the Granada, downhome brand of a pretend Randolph Scott or Gary Cooper. Market days were a swirl of people and animals, transacting and transacted, a theatre of trade, of news exchanged over pints in the busy marketplace pubs.

The future of the Canal looks promising thanks to the efforts of bands of volunteers. The site of the old wharf and basin, though, remains lost in the edgelands. The town Local Plan discourages building on the site in the hope that it will one day be restored, perhaps as a marina. For now, it is another exemplar of civic planning blight in a town, like so many, on an economic downcycle. The Saturday market still lives on though: Dad still goes, odd times – Briggs of Bottesford searching for new bikes for his grandchildren at the Old Wharf sale rooms.

Author and farm cat, 1973

Withamside playground, 1950s

Robbers Rocks, 1950s

Old Joe and young Neil, 1973

Sunday outing, Bob and May, c.1970

Bike sale at the Wednesday market, 1950s

Lipton's grocery, Grandad Bob's workplace, 1938–81

Grandad and a heavy horse, 1940s

Sgt George Holmes, Lincolnshire Regiment, First World War

George and Hettie striding out on their wedding day, 1919

Charles Chalk, c.1920

Amy Chalk, with Lizzie

Chalks' workshop

Charles and Chris, father and son, c.1905

Charles the house-painter

Charles and Chris aboard the Shamrock

Foston farm sisters, 1960s

Barnyard wonderland, the author at North End Farm, 1971

North End Farm and stackyard, early 1950s

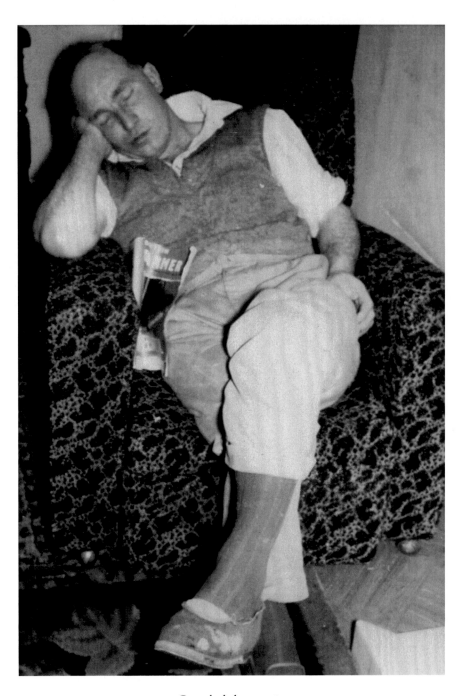

Grandad, late 1960s

Country River

1978
Rainbow Trout at the Foston Ford

My mother's family farmed near the banks of the River Witham on the Lincolnshire–Nottinghamshire border from the 1920s. In the 1970s, I spent so much of my summer holidays rambling over that farm, and in particular to the ford at the riverfield. The village, once a Great North Road staging post, now bypassed and unheeded on a low rise above the dual carriageway, still had many small farms within the parish boundary, the northern limit of which was formed by the line of the river. In its upper reaches, the Witham is the archetypal turbid, sluggish Midland river. A meandering backwater, its slow curve is bottomed with dark clammy mud, the colour of the old clay pipes often turned up by ploughs hereabouts. At the Fallow Lane ford, though, the water is faster-flowing. In summers then, the banks were edged with linen-white sweet briar and dog roses, clumps of alders offering branches for the blue spark of kingfishers. Sparrowhawks weaved through the hawthorn. The long grasses were lathered with cuckoo spit.

At the ford, alterations had been made some time after the war. A wooden footbridge (descendant of a packhorse bridge?) had been replaced with a paint-peeled iron and concrete one and a weir had been built immediately upriver. A depth gauge stood midstream, battered by stones hurled by the village kids in long contests on the bridge. In those days, before the curse of ubiquitous 4x4s, only farm vehicles would cross the ford with alacrity, unless at midsummer when the water levels were lowest. Grandad would truculently dredge some chancers out every year. But one summer holiday trip on the way to Skegness we picked up the grandparents in Dad's 1964 Vauxhall Victor Estate and, weighed down with heavy leather suitcases, our car barely made the crossing, the exhaust pipe catching on a riffle, before a heavy foot on the accelerator span us to the other side. That maggoty old baker's van had a forlorn history, but it's the car of childhood I remember, the Ford-Traverser.

The ford was the village boundary and the frontier of our summer holidays. Beyond was the gravelly shore and the parishes of Westborough, of narrow lanes and Roman ghosts, and Long Bennington by the roaring A1 to Newark and the North, terra incognita to eight-year-olds. But not to cousin N. Several years older, N was tall, good-looking, cool but not stand-offish. He'd roam over to Dry Doddington and Claypole, the bigger villages downriver, on his Raleigh racer to meet the girls he'd laughed with on the double-decker school bus during term time. His jeans made a characteristic swish, the flares whipping the air when he walked. I tried so often to emulate that sound in threadbare hand-me-down cords, but never captured it. He was also a skilled practitioner of the art of playing dead. Tickling, pummelling, shouting down his lugholes: nothing could budge him, until suddenly he'd rise up like a kraken and chase us across the field, bellowing like a bee-stung bull. One time we had played farm cricket in the old dairy and a smashed top-edge had punched a hole in the asbestos roof. We ran off to the river and hid for the day down at the ford where N took us to watch rainbow trout leaping up the weir. He'd be flinging off his trainers and socks, rolling up trouser ends and wading out and up the concrete face, smiling as he tried to catch fish with bare hands. Those iridescent-bellied, spot-finned fish always just eluded him, curvetting away like the dolphins found on Roman brooches in the fields nearby. Those river days shine now, with my mates, stepping out to tiny tapering islands in the stream or lying in the grass watching the rippling waters, wreck-strewn with the sticks and stones we'd cast into them. With N around, all was right with the world. Much later, he left the village, worked in the TV industry, came back long enough for a last falling-out with his folks, and then he was gone and we never saw him again.

By then the ford was long a nexus in our family history, differently coloured for all of us. My father would take long walks down there from the farmhouse on Sundays with his brothers-in-law, escaping the post-prandial family clamour. My mother would walk down to the ford too, other times, with me as a little lad and with Granny, walking the terrier Peg (bought from gypsies as a ratter, hence the inevitable name) or Floss, the redundant collie. At some distance behind too would be the cat, following us unbidden for the stroll, and keeping out of dog-range. Mum would talk about her child days at the ford, summer holidays of cow 'tenting' (tending). She would take the cows down Long Lane to the ford, leaving her sister stationed at the farm end, and the cows would chomp the grasses of the wide roadside verges. Once the cattle had reached the ford, Mum would lead them across to the opposite verge and send them back on their way to the stackyard. This would take all day and happened regularly through the summer months – for Mum this wayside transhumance mostly entailed sitting curled up in the long grass reading Enid Blyton or Louisa May Alcott, only needing to stir to shunt the beasts round again.

My mother could also remember her own grandmother, the redoubtable Granny Holmes, set to hard work in the meadows where the Foston Beck (we are in Viking country) meets the Witham, willows stooping over the river edges, the fields filled with cowslips. They would choose a plot and pick all the flower heads until withy baskets were full, or until the Westborough church bells tolled, the only call for time, a worldly angelus. The flowers were stewed in vats with brewers' yeast, left for the spring to ferment, and tubs of cowslip wine filled the pantry shelves through to the autumn. A few years on, and still only ten years old, Mum would be sent back down to these fields, along the Green Lane, for hay turning and baling in a pre-war gunmetal-grey Ferguson tractor, and then back across an ancient ridge-and-furrow landscape, for centuries unaltered, and past the dark hulking superstructure of a vast wooden barn called the Deauvilles, standing like a vision of a black-masted ship, a rat-ridden East Indiaman perhaps, anchored over swells of wheat and barley.

The Deauvilles was a short distance from the riverfield, scene of the tale of Fred Paley and the bull, a fable worthy of Thomas Hardy. Fred Paley was a yeoman butcher who rarely went down to the riverfield other than to drown kittens in sacks. One day in summer, a few years after the war, he left the slaughter room in a rage about the riverfield gate being left unmended, his smock still streaked with blood. The prize bull was irked, stirred to charge. Its horns gored the butcher, and he died by the ford. His son, my grandfather, remembered his father's hands lying by his side cold and white as knapped flint. He didn't want the bull to be destroyed, but this time yielded to others' opinions. He kept the bull's nose ring though, hanging it from a nail in his workshop for decades after.

I went back to the village recently. Grandad is now dead, the farm sold, the stackyard an executive housing estate, 4x4s in garages made from eighteenth-century bricks reclaimed from the torn-down dovecote. The ridge-and-furrow field has long since been obliterated by industrial agriculture, and the Deauvilles demolished and replaced with a colossal corrugated potato store. I tramped down to the ford with my wife and my mother. The footbridge is still there but the fish had the further obstacle of a burnt out car, joy-ridden up the weir and abandoned. Mantles of keck (cow parsley) and ragwort smothered the banks, but the fishing was strong, although it turns out those rainbow trout of the seventies may have really been highly coloured brown trout and not American interlopers after all.

As Roger Deakin says, rivers are numinous, magical places suffused with memories of childhood. They 'etch time into place', watery worlds, of play pools and testing grounds, on the borders of our childhood lives. Maybe a river runs through all the pictures of our growing up, the youthful rapids to the old-age estuaries. I live in west Dorset now, and the rivers of my own children's play and dreams are chalk streams and winterbournes, swathing through to the fossil coast, then spreading in mini-deltas, like the Wynreford creek that snakes out through the shingle at Seatown, where in the summer kids make dams and dig trenches, and form culverts and tickle fish, and make their own memories.

1934
Man of the Fields

A 1940s ECKO radio now sits on a window ledge in the front room of our house. I salvaged it years ago after it had long gathered dust in grandad's workshop, left there among worm-eaten woodplanes and blunt-toothed saws for a decade or so after the valve had blown. When I was a child, I always liked that old wireless, dark brown Bakelite utilityware but with sinuous Deco flourishes. It sat for years on a red and black formica shelf in the farmhouse kitchen, the bass tones of Radio 4's farming programme echoing through my early morning sleepiness. Grandad would have been up for hours already, out with his flat cap over his line-corrugated bald head, to feed the beasts and size up the day. Then he'd hiss at the cats gathering by the back door, and would come in and sit at the kitchen table. I would watch him eat, *relish*, his breakfast, his ham and English mustard, and then bread with marmalade ladled on to the plate from a yellow china pot. His perfect bovine teeth were gapped between the front two, giving his austere face a rascally slant. Sipping tea 'strong enough to trot a mouse on', he'd stifle a belch, and with a slight raise of his shaggy eyebrows, he'd utter, 'Manners!', to no one in particular. He'd stay till the weather forecast. Inspecting the wireless dial in vain for signs of Radio 1, I'd be caught by the colourful names of the bandwidth positions printed on the perspex pane: Ostend, Amsterdam, Hilversum. . . I asked him where they were: *Holland, boy – good farmers in Holland.*

He'd allowed himself a rare trip away, to Holland, once in the 1960s. A busman's holiday, a coach trip around the tulip fields and a visit to the Delta Scheme sea defence works then under construction after the North Sea floods of 1953, but mostly, on his part, it was a close inspection of Low Country agriculture. Otherwise there'd be the annual trip down south, to the Dorset coast and relations in Lyme and Uplyme, before the long drive home for the harvest season. Saturday afternoons, until the incipient arthritis crocked him, were for cricketing. A stocky long-armed fast-bowler, like Larwood of Notts, and a belligerent lower-order batsman, he would have made a fearsome opponent. As a boy he'd had dreams of going professional, of becoming a Player, of honing his leg-cutters and toe-crunching yorkers at Trent Bridge and round the counties. But his dad wouldn't hear of it, needing him for the farm, and so he became steeped in hard work from an early age, as he would be for near his whole life. His two hundred-acre farm he mostly worked alone, bringing in help at harvest time or with the cattle when need be. It was written on his hands, rough and cracked as a dry riverbed. His asperity came naturally, emeried by the clayey earth he'd shovel day and night digging culverts. I remember being fascinated with his shotguns, kept in the room next to the kitchen, high on the whitewashed wall. The mournful rabbits and pigeons of the upper Withamside never stood a chance.

As the eldest grandson, he had me work on the farm sometimes, in summers stacking bales in the Dutch barns, in winters picking potatoes out of the cold hard ground, thankless tasks I never enjoyed. Wednesday trips to Newark Cattle Market or riding about the farmlands on the back of his open grey Ferguson tractor were more fun. Occasionally, in between bouts of his spectacular swearing, he'd open up and talk about his childhood, a cricket anecdote or school story before his days of hard toiling in the riverfields had begun. One day I was helping him collect logs from the barn. When he was little, grandad said, his mother would throw down logs from the top of the wood pile, and he and his pal Jack North would dodge them for fun, till one day he misjudged and a log hit him on the head and laid him out cold. Another time he told me, he and Jack had once hidden in this barn from Mr Burton, their old headmaster. They'd clambered up the green sides of the stacked wood, Jack snagging the bailer twine that held up his trousers on the way. Their mouths full of sandy dust, they reached the level of the dirt-flecked window, rinsed a little with rain from the afternoon and kept a long watch on the lane below. It was long after milking time, only a dim light flickering through the windowpane and they stayed deep into the cooling August night. They had been running like hares for hours, leading Burton in a merry jig around the village. He'd first spotted them in Jessop's barbershop. Jessop had been waxing on about how they'd both lose their hair young, thick and lustrous though it was now. Staring into the mirror, they'd seen Burton coming up the street, his bow-legged gait bringing forth the barber's usual jibe – 'he'd never stop a pig in a passage'. Throwing a few pennies down on the oily counter, the boys had ran out of the shop towards the river, to the hayrick abandoned midstream, obstacle for the spring trout and plaything of the village lads. 'Bald by twenty, you'll see boys, not be giving me much business,' the barber's words curled behind them. Old Burton was no match in speed but he was dogged, and they knew why he wanted them. The boys had spent most of the summer in trouble, for tying together the girls' pigtails, for kicking lads' shins, for skiving off to go fishing from the hayrick's bench seat. They had taken the cane every day for two months; then were set to working the headmaster's garden. They had worked in the shade of a horse chestnut, sleeves rolled up to the elbows, tending and watering until swallows dipped round the bean poles. The garden was Burton's delight. On the last night of school grandad and Jack had stolen back after dark, dug up all the asters and peonies, cut them off at the roots, and replanted them. They had all withered before the next sundown.

Jack was now long dead, killed in the army truck he was driving at the Sicily landings; best job he'd ever had, he'd said, like 'barrowing daylight into a dark passage'. Grandad had stayed home on the farm, his imperious father throwing his RAF call-up papers on the fire. Two years after the war, his father had been killed by his own prize bull in a sodden field next to the Witham, and the farm was thrust onto grandad, a young man left standing alone. Part of the farm holding was the house next to the school, where Headmaster Burton still lived, and who so became his tenant, and at the mercy of eviction papers grandad would never serve. He married my grandmother, had five daughters, and spent his life a man of the fields. Did he ever listen to that old radio, Test matches from Lords and Melbourne, and think of a different path? He would never say.

1940

The Whistling Soldier

George shivered. He had taken again to his bathchair, parked up at the bottom of the garden beneath two drowsy willows on the bank of the river. He hadn't meant to nod off but the old lung trouble had flared up again and he was heavy with the fatigue of war work. During the Great War he had snatched sleep between the raids on no-man's-land, or in the lulls of heavy shelling, curled up in himself at the foot of dugouts. Now another war had come and the country was tense with expectation: would this be the invasion summer? But today the cleansing riverine air had swept him away in a dream-laden sleep.

The sun-filled afternoon had drained away and the light was beginning to scatter over the fields to Fulbeck Heath. He stretched a little and, lifting his flat cap, ran a hand through his wire-brush hair. He couldn't yet stir himself from this comforting spot, from the wool shawl bound tightly over his knees. Or surrender his daydreams. It had all come back, the first time he'd been here, to Hester's parents' smallholding by this kink in the river, soon after demob in 1919. The sun had been hot and high, mocking the winters of the past four years. Poppies and oxeye daisies massed on the bankside. Hettie had been bathing in the river, her long plaited auburn hair trailing on the surface, gleaming in the watery light. She looked like a peasant Ophelia, but was carefree, happy as she talked quietly to George while she swam. They had married that summer, after a long engagement. George had been her 'Soldier Boy Jock', as he styled himself in letters home: the army knew him as 3052 Lance Corporal GW Holmes, 4th Lincolnshire Regiment, 138 Infantry Brigade, 46 North Midland Division, British Expeditionary Force. He'd joined up in early '15 on the swell of national fervour; then basic training at Luton and so to France, where soon enough his 'head was a mass of mud'. The regiment had then been ordered to Alexandria, Egypt, a pointless venture not long enough for a breath of Mediterranean air; soon they were back to the mires of Flanders. He'd got scarce a scratch throughout though, only a cigarette shot out of his mouth by a sniper near Rouen. But in March 1918, the Lincolnshire Regiment reduced to bare bones, he was taken prisoner of war and sent to a barbed-wire stalag in Germany. His family heard nothing of him, fearing the worst. After 11 November, the guards had simply opened the camp gates and George and his ragged pals walked out and kept on walking, all the way to the coast.

That walk haunted him. Its legacy was the tuberculosis he had been stricken with; at one point they had sheltered for days in the collapsed cellar of a former farmhouse, the prison cough they all shared barking out in the night over the frozen, now silent, fields. And, worse, the real freight of the war, memories of the pals who hadn't made it, those who'd had 'gone west', ravaged with the bulk of a generation. He'd sent a telegram home from the troop ship bringing him back to England and a muted homecoming – his mother had died just an hour before he arrived home. Hester had nursed him and they'd spent long curative afternoons down by the river, but the TB had meant spells away at a bracing sanatorium in Yorkshire, and long intervals of incapacity in the bathchair. His bakery business had failed, his lungs not able to withstand the floury atmosphere of the bread ovens. The campaign medals stayed in the drawer – he said they may as well have been made of putty.

Somehow, though, his optimism hadn't been snagged on the barbed wire of the Western Front. He thought back to when he and Hettie had had the chance to go to Canada, to work on his uncle's farm on the vast prairies of Manitoba. Three of his sisters had gone to Australia after all. But his roots were too deep and tangled here in the English Midlands, and it did seem life could begin anew in the lanes and villages beside the Witham. He simply chose to write over the past, on the palimpsest of the life lived before the war. They had made the best of their second chance.

George could hear children running and playing and hollering in the fields beyond the church. It brought back the best of days, when his son and daughter had been small, when they would climb up the braked wheel and into the bathchair with him and nap on his wheezy chest. Later they'd have swimming parties in the river, togged out in homespun outfits and he'd entertain them with songs and stories and his fluting whistling that always made them laugh. On long summer nights when he felt well, they would all cross the river at the watering hole where they drew water for washing and walk to Westborough, to the little parlour pub called the Blue Greyhound, for a half of bitter-shandy, or a teatime treat. When the house upriver at Marston had been lost, they'd come back here to Hettie's folks. They bought an old Nissen hut from Belton army camp, a former hospital, costing £60 including delivery on a pantechnicon, and erected it in sections on his in-laws' small plot of land. The construction took weeks – it had been hard work for a weakened man. His brother-in-law Frank, Uncle Lol from Derbyshire and Mr Newton, the deaf former miner from across the road, had dug out the foundations, raised the frame, shingled the roof and insulated the hut with sheets of asbestos. Their water came direct from the Witham, heated in copper-bottomed pails, and the cold winter winds driving off the North Sea and across the Fens had only to be withstood until they could afford encasing the homestead in brick. They'd all lived there comfortably, finding contentment where it could be found.

A breeze was getting up, riffling the waters of the river. The evening swallows had begun to flit over the surface. A single star was slung in the sky over far-off Lincoln and the RAF stations, tied in the ribbons of contrails. George knew he had to raise himself up out of the bathchair. He was due for the nightshift at the munitions factory in town. It irked him that the foreman let him and the other old soldiers clock-off early so they could make the bus stop unjostled. So it goes for the old ones, he thought. The wind was singing through the long grass on the far bank, a high flat whistle. It was time to go.

For my great-grandfather George William Holmes (1893–1967)

1919
Old Bones

The river was still and black. It was late September now and the summer had been packed away with the last of the apples. A fog was skulking in from over the mudstones of the Vale of Belvoir, thin and watery and secluding.

Charles Chalk was smiling as he leant on the creaking gate, Toby, his terrier, watchful at his side. He had changed out of his decorating overalls, and looked dapper in a pressed white Irish linen shirt, black corduroy jacket and trilby hat. Pipe smoke swirled into his eyes and his thick grey moustache twitched as he moved the stem along with his teeth. He was watching the lame horse in the paddock by the riverside, a chestnut mare with some dappling at the withers. The horse was gamely cantering despite her bony spavins, steam rising off her back. Some char-black crows were screeching over the field, flying low on the feed, avoiding the mare, but agitating her enough to make her lumber towards the riverbank. Charles's wife Amy, still in her work smock, her white hair swept back, her hands gnarled and arthritic, was uttering soft injunctions while she threw kitchen slops in the direction of the old sow they called Lizzy, who was rootling outside the shed.

Charles remembered how Chris, his and Amy's eldest, had always been a good hand with the animals. As a small boy he'd rig up the goat to pull the child's carriage Charles had built for him one Christmas, and career round the lanes and up to the churchyard, where the goat would chomp wayside burdock and cow parsley. It had been Chris who had tended the farm horses, staying up all night with the skewbald that had pneumonia one moonless February. He'd known all the names of the birds and riverside blooms and insects skittering on the surface or on the wing. On sunny Sundays, Charles and Chris would row down the Witham to do some idle fishing between smokes in the boat they had built together, the Shamrock, a sleek, deep-green skiff, knocked up between sessions building the coffins that as village undertakers they were often called on to make.

Charles had had Chris on his mind all day, a day of grim anniversary. The war had been over for ten months, but Chris would never make old bones. He had long been lying in Dud Corner, a cemetery in the Pas-de-Calais, named for the host of unexploded enemy shells found there. He had joined the cavalry at the war's start, but a farm boy's disgust at the treatment and slaughter of the horses had led to his transfer to the infantry. He had been killed on the second day of the Battle of Loos on 26 September 1915, drowned in a haze of chlorine gas, four years ago to the day. He never met his infant son Ron, born weeks after his death.

The day was falling away as the mists rolled in. Clouds the texture of sifted flour rumbled across the western sky. Charles shuffled off to the barn to paint in oils, a small canvas for his own pleasure, as he did most evenings. Landscapes were his chosen form – he would sit and recall the soft folds of his Hampshire youth, the pebbly chalk streams, the abundant woodlands, the homely fields. He always painted a version of the same scenes, culled from the memory of the walk from his home near Southampton to London in 1877. He had been seventeen years old, and not the first to stride out towards the clamouring city, or the last. His father, who had never held out hopes for his son's prospects, gave him sixpence for the trip and didn't wait at the door to see him off. Charles marched out one midsummer morning, a crust of bread in his pocket and a bag of tools on his back, sleeping in haylofts on the way, earning small change from doing odd jobs on downland farms, a cheery vagabond. He relished the nights, alone after years in his folks' briny, cramped cottage near the docks of Southampton Water. He thought back now to those nights, spent scanning the skies, the old shambling cavalcade of stars, fuel of pure hopes, limitless desires, moments rich with shining possibilities.

London, of course, had been full of wonder and dubious bargains, as it always had and will be. Soon enough he found himself apprenticed to a firm of Putney painters and decorators, and it had been while learning his trade that he'd met Amy Harrison, daughter of a Lincolnshire shepherd and now in service as the laundress in a grand house next to the Thames. They married in the spring of 1883 and lived in Fulham for some years, where their two boys, Chris and Frank, were born. Then in 1887, Amy's father died of appendicitis. Amy and Charles appealed to the landlord, the Earl of Ancaster, to take over the tenancy of her father's small farm at Kirkby Underwood on the Rippingale Fen, south Lincolnshire. But the landowner would not countenance such an agreement with the mere daughter of his tenant and Charles and Amy and family were forced to find lodging in town, where Charles once again set up as house decorator. Eventually, they had saved enough to buy their own smallholding with a bankside garden, ten miles downriver, where the Witham begins its curve north through the clayey Trent Vale.

Charles opened the tall wooden doors to the barn and

inched past the two-wheeled trap and into his workshop. He lit the stove and sat easily at the grooved bench. The back of the wormy timber door was daubed with colour tests, the paints he'd mixed from white bases and a panoply of chalky pigments for the walls of a humble kitchen or a grand drawing room – he was known to be able to match any shade, often brought to him on patches of cloth or old china pots. He turned to the canvas, a sketch of a small lonely cottage on the edge of a cornfield, in the style of Samuel Palmer or John Constable. He drew on his pipe and his mind wrapped around the idea of negative space, the line where air meets the hard edge of what is real, the marbled endpaper sky above the cottage in his painting. After a while, his pipe went out as his thoughts came back to Chris, off in that far country.

1995

North End

In the dairy an ancient bulb was hanging from a thin braided cord, rimed in straw dust and casting a buttery half-light. I walked through the main atrium, behind the feed stalls and into an anteroom, remembering how as a small child I'd seek out my grandfather in here as he checked his account books, his eyes grave, his face set hard. The stores in those days were stacked high with bags of cow cake and fertiliser, each as solid as a man; metal pails brimming over with chicken feed; galvanised iron ten-gallon milk churns embossed with the emblem for the Co-operative Wholesale Society; giant cans of Swarfega and tubs of creosote. Today the smell was the same – flue gases and turned milk and antique raked-up muck. But now that windowless room was mainly empty. Accretions of cold dust were finely layered over some rickety spindle-backed chairs as if blown in on the wind. Old corn ears littered the concrete floor. A rusty tobacco tin, where grandad had kept his strapless wristwatch, poked out from the pocket of some worn-out overalls hung on a nail next to a curling 1980s feedstock company calendar annotated in biro capitals. Fantastical cobwebs looped in the high corners, tensed by the husks of dead flies. As I stood there in the draughty doorway the bulb fizzed and sputtered out and the other lights in the dairy cut out too – they were wired in series like Christmas illuminations. A shaft of grey daylight laddered down from a gap in the roof and I made my way through the empty corridors and outside again.

The notices had appeared in the *Journal* and the *Advertiser*. After seventy years North End farm was up for sale. The machinery plant and tools had been sold off the year before, some still operational and now seeing service on other local farms, others outmoded and destined to adorn gastropubs, providing some faux rustic colour above new inglenook fireplaces. Ancient pantiles from an old barn had been bought by an American dealer and were now roofing a granary restaurant in rural Illinois. The tarnished and blunted blades of a plough could still be seen amongst some rank fireweed, like the scapulas of a once sleek earth-moving creature. The stackyard, the last in the village on the lane to the river, was stilled. Rainwater lay in stagnant puddles on the uneven ground. Tall spindles of grass and some wanton wheat sprouted in shadeless corners, as close-packed as a cornfield.

My grandparents were readying themselves for the last auction, to bear witness to their lives going up for sale. My grandfather Ted was in his seventies and bent with arthritis. The farm work was now a tough daily grind that he would have endured till he could no longer stand, but he felt the old country attributes of hard work and patience were no longer enough in an era of paper mountains, aggressive marketing and diminishing returns. My grandmother Mary, though, was full of memories, and more sentimental about leaving the farmstead: it had been a life of hard graft and thrift, but she'd give her cheerful bosomy shrug and produce one of her gnomic sayings: 'We're not short of what we've got.' She hated to see the place decay, to look, as she said, like 'The Wreck of the Hesperus'. For her, the farm still echoed with the clatter of children: her five daughters, now grown and married, the two lost infant sons, and the hordes of grandchildren. She had been in her element during the big family gatherings, the Sunday teas, served through the hatch to the farmhouse dining room, overlooked by the ascending line of wedding photographs. Plates were arrayed over the table on a white tablecloth: ham and cold cuts of beef, pickled onions and English cheeses, salad tomatoes, radishes, beetroots, spring onions with salt. Everyone had thick slabs of white bread and butter, cups of tea all round. The smallest cousins sat on poufs at the coffee table, ignoring the babble of the grown-ups at the big table. For pudding were cakes and trifles, wondrous confections – even with full stomachs most of us had a little of everything. Afterward some of the older ones walked to the ford, or talked by the farm gate. Most lolled on sofas. Grandad would have his hair cut in the kitchen, the washing up piling up around him. And then it was time for home, effusive kisses, bear hugs, and time for a catnap in the back of car going down the night-time A1. My grandmother would miss all this the most.

I had come back to the farm to make a self-conscious final tour of my childhood imaginarium, a micro-landscape I knew so well, ghosts behind every barn door. I turned right out of the dairy and went over to the water tower, a lofty grey structure topped with black bowsers for irrigating the arable fields and cattle troughs. Under the tower, amongst the nest of iron supports, was the kennel where a succession of farm dogs had lived, never allowed in the farmhouse and not kept as pets. I feared them as a small boy, their exuberant jumpiness when released from their captivity or the look of frustration in their mustelid eyes when tethered, their hot slavering mouths full of long yellow teeth. To escape their attentions I would stand on the stone blocks where the milk churns were placed ready for the delivery van, waiting for the kennel door to latch again.

I climbed a few rungs of the water tower ladder. From

here I could see the small coterie of young trees leaning into each other next to the wooden fence, including the horse chestnut I'd planted when I was five, and that had now outgrown me three to one. Beyond was the homefield, the farmyard's yawning hinterland, and the edge of the slurry pond dug out singlehandedly by grandad long ago. The homefield was broad and flat, short-cropped and sheltered from the wind by old hedgerows – it could have served as an aerodrome in a county of so many. In fact, it was here that Uncle Ian, after spending weeks assembling, painting, oiling and balancing, had presented the maiden flight of a remote-controlled model airplane. All the grown-ups and grandchildren had gathered by the pond, the mood festive, the day bright; calibrations and calculations and last-minute checks heightened the expectation. Finally, a lever was pulled, a button pushed, a connection made. The plane revved into life, tracked across the pasture and lifted off the ground in a petrol-fumy jolt. The glory of a successful launch: cheers rang out from the young ones. And then the plane seemed suddenly to pick up speed, as if in a fit of pique. Uncle Ian grappled with the controls, his roll-up wilting at the side of his mouth. The plane flew off over the rooftops towards the river, a rogue drone, never to be seen again.

Grandad had been working down at the riverfield and had missed the air show, but caught a glimpse of the model plane's serene progress over Lincoln Hill. Perhaps as he dug out a ditch with the heavy iron shovel, his mind's eye made a jump-cut. In 1941, as he worked in the homefield, he had watched a fleet of German bombers, Heinkels, fly over towards the town ten miles away. He heard later there had been a raid on the munitions factory. Joyce, a girl he had been courting over the last year, had just come off the dayshift. She was one of forty-one killed. He never talked about it thereafter.

At the homefield edge ran the beck, and alongside was a favourite nook, a hollow by a sycamore tree, an ideal den. I spent days here under big skies, reading books not on the school list: Chandler and Kerouac, Laurie Lee and Alain Fournier. Or else there'd be hours of languid talk with cousins and brothers, or of woolgathering with my back against the tree, eyeing the spiders climbing to the tip of the grasses and then waiting for a gust to launch into the wind. I was replete with the time all ahead of me and mostly oblivious of the greater world beyond. But even here in this sequestered spot the crank of history was turning and it wasn't long before national politics began to burn into my hazy consciousness. During the 1984 strike, three miners down from the Nottinghamshire pits were caught poaching by the beck. The colliers had been seized by the police on an autumn night as the strike bit hard, hunched in black overcoats, out for a pheasant or rabbit, slim pickings in their night-time wanderings. My grandfather, a true-blue Tory his whole life, surprised me with his sympathy – Sunday teatimes always ended in debates about the state of the world and he knew I was forming the leftward convictions I've held ever since. He pressed no charges against the miners, although there were others that did.

A few years on, I squandered exquisite woeful hours here yearning over the girl from a neighbouring farm I'd met while potato-picking one winter. She wore snug-fit jeans, had a short bob of curly russet hair and had an exotic air of knowingness, of Romany independence. I'd seen her once walking the footpaths of the Viking Way that ran down here towards the river at Marston Hall, and I always hoped to see her here again. I never did. At last, a couple of years later I saw her at a teenage party. She was sat on the stairs weeping and I, still too shy to talk to her, could only walk outside and feel sorry for both of us.

An old hose stood limp by the cattle byre. Past the turnstile gate, the reek of dried manure still hung in the air. How many beasts passed through here during the farm's life, their hooves clattering on broken-brick ground? In the 1960s grandad bought most of his stock from Scotland. They would be sent south by train and he would collect them at the halt station at Sedgebrook, and walk them the five miles to the farm via Allington and over the Great North Road, the A1, stalling traffic to Leeds and London on either lane. Behind the central courtyard, where the cattle overwintered, was the crew yard, the site of calf longboxes, brick pens and sheds for calving and rearing youngsters. Adjoining that was the double-storey bullpen, with a ladder for outside access and spy-window for looking down on the bull, a caution no doubt inspired by family history, our own old testament fable, the death of grandad's father trampled by his own prize animal. I recalled now the boyhood thrill of climbing the ladder and peering through the window and into the abysmal depth of the bull's eyes.

I didn't venture into the empty byres but walked through the open, skeletal Dutch barns erected in the seventies. A few relic straw bales, faded and fibrous, were stacked in a corner. Here the heavy plant used to be stored, the treacherous-looking threshing machine superseded by a pillar-box red combine, and the hulking modern Canadian tractors. Sometimes during harvest time grandad would have me up in the cab with him, where he'd have Test Match Special loud on the radio as we swathed through corn like West Indian bowlers through English batsmen. Grandad had a particular affinity for 'Fiery' Fred Trueman, former Yorkshire and England fast bowler, then self-styled sage of the commentary box. He shared his conservative politics, a certain bloody-minded estimation of modern mores and the odd distinction of them both weighing in at an eye-watering 14 pounds at birth.

The familiar unvarying cooing of collared doves brought me back into the stackyard. The wooden door to a storeroom was opposite, once painted red and now washed out to a peeling pink. In front of this door I used to haul a large plastic drum, makeshift stumps for games of barnyard cricket with my cousins. The batsmen's aim was to smite the ball into the haystacks and watch the fielders scurry over the bales in search of it; or better, a long straight hit over the farm gates and into Fallow Lane, a lordly six-and-out. Only miscues to the offside were discouraged – here were the glasshouses, some days the tempting sector of brinkmanship and bravado, but usually a glinting minefield, like the wrath of grandad, best avoided. Sometimes grandad would watch and encourage from the sidelines, throwing in mystifying references from his own youth: 'that was a Denis Compton shot' or 'that turned a mile, a real Hedley Verity'. Once he was persuaded to turn his arm over, which he did with a hard-won smile, but the gnawing joint pain was all too visible and he soon wandered off to the greenhouses, all economy of movement and expression. Cricket provided our common language and hunting ground – we could meet out in the middle and nowhere else.

I noticed that the tendrils of a climbing plant had curled up the panes of the greenhouses. These had been an extension of the farm garden, something like what the ancients called the hortus, well worked and manured ground that my grandparents worked hard to make tidy and decorous as well as productive and fruitful. During the war, and for some time after, Italian prisoners worked on the local farms, replacing villagers who had left to join up or work in armament factories. Grandad had two men from Liguria help him in the rationing years – watering those feeble sun-starved tomatoes and staking out the bean poles, how must they have dreamed of succulent zucchini, sweet bell peppers, bunches of aromatic basil and rosemary for remembrance.

Moving on, I went over to the chicken huts, part hidden behind high nettles. Some of the huts were on corroded wheels from the time when they'd be repositioned across fields to provide an even composting. There was also a large corrugated poultry shed, another place of terror for me as a young boy, the roosters seeming as tall as me in their strutting cocksureness, their beaks angular and quick to peck, their faces an angry red – I would hide timorously behind my grandmother's skirt as she fed them from the pail, and silently sympathise with the bantams cowering in the rafters. Grandad once told me he long ago knew a chimney sweep who used to send live chickens down smokestacks, their panicked flapping dislodging soot on the descent, but I never knew if he was pulling my leg.

Behind the huts was the wall of locally made bricks with stone copings, and a tall wooden fence with a gate to the neat cottage where my mother had grown up. Next to the wall was the former dovecote and workshop, eighteenth-century vernacular buildings and survivors from a previous farm. Here grandad stored tools and old brass collars from the pre-tractor age of heavy horses, and engreased spare parts for long-scrapped Fergusons and Fordsons. In here he would also make cack-handed tool repairs on a splintery bench lined with woodworm like an Arabic script. Everything had been neatly arranged on the Georgian dresser with Greek key mouldings or from hooks in the unplastered wall, a hymn to orderliness, a reflection of grandad's daily stubborn wrestle with nature and life in general. Now there was a general air of dereliction, as if the mellowed bricks knew they'd soon be demolished to red dust.

I walked on and peered into the corrugated Land Rover shed, though the 1960s vintage model had been sold off years before. I remembered the gaps in the canvas that someone said were bullet holes. Opposite was the old granary and drying shed, where the harvested corn was deposited late summer nights, the air fizzing with chaff in the headlights. The dryer was a hot, seed-cloaked, echoic place at harvest time and it was here that the epic battles with rats played out – I remembered seeing the dead ones lying by the wall, electrocuted after chewing through armoured cables. This was the earnest business end of farm toil – for grandad, happiness was a full grain store and a good price at market. Now the shed was an empty shell, the windsock sagging against the wall.

That last day in 1995, I leant on the five-bar gates, my back against the hand-painted North End Farm sign, and looked over the ghost of a cricket pitch that my grandfather had bestrode in the forties and fifties, long since ploughed up into another solemn field. Small farms were dying all over the country, victims of food and health scares and agglomerating big business. I wondered if grandad would be left another chuntering old farmer in an overheated bungalow, a rambling rose round the front door and a fish pond out back. In the weeks before leaving North End I remembered the day he discovered a mass of ants in the living room carpet, carried in on a flower pot. He worked himself up into a frenzy, manically hoovering up the ants, and then burning the dust bag out in the yard, a strange crematory rite that summed up so much of his attitude to the nature he had spent his life working with, or battling against. By this time, I had left the area, gone to college and settled in the South – as Richard Benson says in his memoir *The Farm*, I had long felt here like the village idiot with O-levels. And although I had been desperate to escape the loneliness of my homeland, I still felt a strong place-attachment to the farm's sturdy topography of work and play and the joy of its open country, in a time out of time. One summer when I was staying at the farm, aged around eight or nine, my grandmother woke me in the middle of the night and beckoned me to the window. Over towards the river the sky was a ragged fluorescent lightshow, roving waves of blue-green radiance in a sea of cold white stars. We stood for a long time, imprinting the shared experience, the Northern Lights rarely seen at this latitude. But in the morning the sky was deadbeat and unravelled, the colour of cut hay. This last time at the farm had the same numbness. For all the encrustations of time, all seemed weightless, made only of smoke, and those days seemed done.

A near two decades have since followed and thoughts of my happy childhood and lonesome adolescence have receded as I watch my children seek out their own touchstones, their elemental places, to run and play in the fields and by the rivers three hundred miles south-west, on days of sun and rain, where sky and water meet.

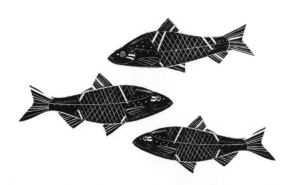

Acknowledgements

The pieces in this book started life on the gem of a web space that is Caught by the River, curated by Jeff Barrett, Robin Turner and Andrew Walsh. Jeff in particular has been a great friend and mentor to these writings, and this book owes its existence to him.

Thanks also to:

Jonathan Gibbs for the cover illustrations; Carol Briggs and Little Toller for the book's design and production; and Alex Friedman for help with the photographs.

Richard Benson for the foreword.

My friends Ziyad Marar, Mila Steele, Craig Smith, Roy McMillan and Nick Bellorini for far more than barroom encouragement.

My parents Janet and Robin Sentance, for the family lore.

My children Evie and Noah.

My wife Kate, for the belief, and the love.

Published by Caught by the River & Little Toller Books in 2014

Text © Neil Sentance 2014

The right of Neil Sentance to be identified as the author of this work has been asserted by him in accordance with Copyright, Design and Patents Act 1988

Jacket and chapter illustrations © Jonathan Gibbs 2014

Typeset in Garamond by Carol Briggs & Little Toller Books

Printed in Great Britain by TJ International Ltd, Padstow, Cornwall

All papers used by Caught by the River and Little Toller Books are natural, recyclable products made from wood grown in sustainable, well-managed forests

A catalogue record for this book is available from the British Library

ISBN 978-1-908213-23-5